Christopher Columbus and the Discovery of the Americas

By Doug West, Ph.D.

Christopher Columbus and the Discovery of the Americas
By Doug West, Ph.D.

ISBN: 9798672685045

Table of Contents

Preface

Welcome to the book, *Christopher Columbus and the Discovery of the Americas*. This book is volume 47 of the 30 Minute Book Series and, as the name of the series implies, if you are an average reader this book will take less than an hour to read. Since this short book is not meant to be an all-encompassing biography of Christopher Columbus, you may want to know more about the man and his discoveries. To help you with this, there are several good references at the end of this book. I have also provided a Timeline, in order to link together the important events of his life, and a section titled "Biographical Sketches," which includes brief biographies of some of the key individuals in the book.

Thank you for purchasing this book, and I hope you enjoy your time reading about the explorer who discovered the Americas.

Doug West
July 2020

DOUG WEST, Ph.D.

Introduction

For the last five centuries the name Christopher Columbus has been synonymous with the discovery of the Americas. However, recent evidence has come to light that reveals he was not the first European to set foot in North America; rather, Viking explorers appeared during the tenth century. About A.D. 985 an Icelander named Erik the Red colonized the west coast of a cold and desolate island he deceptively called Greenland. About a year later, a trader mistakenly sailed past Greenland and spotted land further west, prompting Leif Erikson, son of Erik the Red, to sail west out from Greenland in about A.D. 1001. He landed in a place he called "Vinland," because of all the grape vines he found, which is now the Canadian providence of Newfoundland. Erikson and his fellow explorers attempted to settle in this new country, but their settlement only lasted a few years. As the story goes, the natives were hostile and greatly outnumbered the Norsemen.

Up until the 1960s, the story of the Vikings' first landing in North America was the stuff of legends. This all changed in 1960 when the Norwegian husband and wife team of Helge and Anne Ingstad discovered the remains of a Norse village at L'Anse aux Meadows on the northern tip of the island of Newfoundland. Over the next several years, the Ingstads and a group of international archeologists uncovered the foundations of eight separate buildings belonging to these early settlers, thus firmly establishing the presence of Vikings in North America over one thousand years ago.

Figure – Full scale replica of a Viking longship that is similar to what Leif Erikson used to cross the Atlantic Ocean.

It would be over four hundred years after the colony of Vinland was abandoned before Europeans would once again visit this new continent. The refinement of maritime navigation technology and the improvement of ships in the fifteenth century allowed adventurous sailors to travel great distances for trade and plunder. The rise of the age of discovery coincided with the growth of trade, cities, and modern corporations.

Exploration was also spurred by the rise of nation states, ruled by kings and queens who had the authority and money to sponsor explorers in search of plunder. Along with the growth of centralized power came the development of a merchant class who needed uniform currencies, trade laws, and the elimination of trade barriers to expand trade with other nation states.

The resurgence of scientific inquiry and the renaissance of art and literature were forces shaping the world. Learned men and women were beginning to no longer rely on the old dogma of the church and ancient philosophers; they started to question the world through the eyes of rational inquiry. The printing press with movable type, invented by Johannes Guttenberg around 1440, further quickened the speed of change. This transformative invention allowed books full of knowledge to be printed and distributed throughout much of the civilized world.

The age of discovery was especially influenced by the ancient knowledge of geography. The Pythagoreans, Greek philosophers from the sixth century B.C., had taught that the earth was round and by the third century B.C. the earth's size was calculated close to modern values. An educated European from the fifteenth century was taught that the earth was round, though some still believed it was flat.

With the revival of the pursuit of science came progress in the art of navigation. Mariners began to use new instruments to sight the stars, allowing them to determine their latitude. Measuring the height of the North Star above the horizon allowed a ship's captain to determine their latitude with some degree of accuracy. Knowing a ship's longitude was a much bigger problem because it required knowing the longitude where you started, the exact time of travel, direction, and the speed of the ship through the water, which was measured using a chip log. The chip, a small piece of wood, was attached to a light rope on a reel. Knots were tied at 47' 3" intervals, and the distance a line would be pulled out of the reel in 28 seconds indicated the ship's speed in knots; a speed of one knot allowed the ship to travel one nautical mile in an hour. Time for the 28 second interval was measured with a 14 or 28 second sand glass. Thus, a navigator could measure the ship's speed through the water by the number of knots rolled out before the sandglass expired. The compass was also a necessary instrument for the fifteenth century navigator, pointing the direction of north when the North Star was not visible. The variation between the true north pole and the magnetic north pole was just starting to be understood in the time of the early explorers. The passage of time was normally measured in a crude fashion with an hour sand glass. On fair days, time keeping errors could be corrected by observing the moment the sun reached the zenith; that is, the highest point overhead. Knowing all this information gave the navigator the ship's approximate position on the globe.

Into this world where ideas and knowledge were evolving rapidly was born a man who would change the face of the earth, Christopher Columbus. Though the memory of Columbus has been tarnished by his harsh treatment of native peoples, his story of discovery will be told for generations to come.

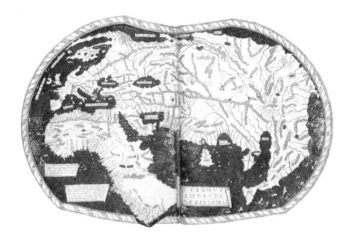

Figure - The world map, ca. 1489, by Heinrich Hammer. Note the large size of Asia and the lack of North and South America.

Chapter 1 - The Early Life of Christopher Columbus

"Lying on a feather mattress or quilt will not bring you renown." – Leonardo Da Vinci

The city of Genoa, situated on the western coast of modern Italy, was one of the largest cities in Europe in the middle of the fifteenth century–rivaling London, Paris, or Venice. The port city bustled with trade from distant towns that dotted the coast of the Mediterranean Sea. The city had many restrictions on its citizens; on the way they dressed, prostitution, and how much they could spend on luxury items. "Girls with a candle," as prostitutes were known, got the name because they regulated their time with clients by the flickering of a small candle. They were forbidden from entering a church or cemetery and had to wear an insignia on their clothes announcing their profession. In families with enough money to keep their daughters out of prostitution, usually when the young lady reached fifteen, often she was given to her new husband in an arranged marriage. Slavery was an integral part of Genoese society; even modest families had one or two female slaves. Though Christianity prohibited bondage, exceptions were made for non-Christian slaves, Russian, Arab, Mongol, Bulgarian, and Chinese. Slaves were mere property and their ownership was formal, deeded, and notarized. The economic and social life of the city centered around the sea. When times were good, the markets near the port hummed with the activity of merchants selling fish, fruits, vegetables, spices, cloth, household goods, and anything else they could turn into a profit. The artisan class of Genoa were the sailmakers, caulkers, coopers, carpenters, lantern makers, and other trades that centered around building and maintaining ships. It was in this place that young Christopher Columbus would learn to see the world through the eyes of a Genoese and take to the sea at a young age.

Christopher Columbus was born sometime between August 25 and the end of October 1451 in the city of Genoa, in present day Italy. He was born into a working-class family in which his father, Domenico Colombo, was a wool weaver, a tavern keeper, and also owned a cheese stand where his young sons sometimes worked as helpers. Christopher was the eldest of five children. Two of his brothers, Bartholomew and Diego, would later be involved in his voyages of discovery. As a young man, Christopher worked with his father and learned the trade of wool weaving. Like most commoners of the day, he received little if any formal education. On his own he learned Latin, which allowed him to pursue his thirst for knowledge about the ocean and distant lands. He later learned to speak Spanish and Portuguese through living and traveling in Spain and Portugal.

Columbus felt the call of the sea at an early age. Genoa was a leading port city for trading and a center for sailors and map makers for all of Europe. Living near the sea, he would take short trips along the coast during time off from his father's shop. In May 1476, Columbus sailed--probably as a deck hand--in a Genoese armed convoy bound for the coast of England. Off the coast of Portugal near Cape St. Vincent, the fleet was attacked by French privateers. During the intense battle, Columbus's ship sank and he was wounded, forcing him to swim six miles to the Portuguese shore. Washing up on shore, penniless, he made his way to Lisbon where he found some of his fellow Genoese countrymen and recovered from his wounds.

While living in Lisbon, Columbus's younger brother Bartholomew came to live with him. An acquaintance of Bartholomew at the time described him as a " hawker of printed books, who carried on his trade in the land of Andalusia," and a "man of great intelligence though with little book learning, very skilled in the art of cosmography and the mapping of the world." Bartholomew set up business in Lisbon as a map dealer with Christopher as his partner.

Christopher went back to sea again in the winter of 1476 to 1477, sailing to Galway in Ireland and then possibly to Iceland. Before returning to Lisbon, he sailed north toward Jan Mayen Island. In the summer of 1478, he sailed to Madeira Island as a purchasing agent for the Genoese firm of Negro and Centurione. During these years, Columbus became an excellent seaman, learning much about the patterns of the wind, sea, and navigation.

While attending mass one Sunday, Columbus noticed a young woman of about twenty. Her name was Felipa Moniz Perestrello, and she was the daughter of a distinguished family who had been active in the colonization of the island of Madeira. Though details of their courtship are virtually non-existent, his son Ferdinand would later extol the virtue of his father: "In as much as he behaved very honorably, and was a man of such fine presence, and withal so honest, that she became his wife." Columbus apparently went with his wife to live on the Island of Porto Santo off the coast of Spain, possibly working as a merchant. It was there that his son Diego was born in 1479 or 1480. By this time, Columbus was a tall, white haired, pious man who had become an experienced mariner, mastering the art and science of navigation at sea. Years later, his son Ferdinand wrote a description of his father: "The admiral was a well-built man of more than average stature, the face long, the cheeks somewhat high, his body neither fat nor lean. He had an aquiline nose and light-colored eyes; his complexion too was light and tending to bright red. In youth his hair was blond, but when he reached the age of thirty, it all turned white."

Figure - Portrait of Christopher Columbus by Sebastiano del Piombo in 1519. No known authentic portraits of Columbus exist.

Enterprise of the Indies

Possibly during a trip to the Portuguese trading post of São Jorge da Mina on the Gold Coast of Africa, Columbus began to speculate on the possibility of sailing westward to reach Asia. His son Ferdinand later wrote of his father's dream, "that if the Portuguese could sail so far south, it should be possible to sail as far westward, and that it was logical to expect to find land in that direction." As he read more of the ancient texts, Columbus became more convinced that his idea of reaching the Orient by sailing west was possible. His idea had real commercial value as European demand was strong for Eastern teas and spices, and the only available route for obtaining these goods was a lengthy land journey by caravan. The idea was not novel to Columbus, but he worked diligently to realize his dream. His "Enterprise of the Indies," as it came to be known, made financial sense if only a sea path could be found to the riches of Asia. To the deeply religious Columbus, who planned on converting many to Christianity, it was a plan truly ordained by God.

To pursue his dream he needed ships, a crew, and money. Since he was living in Portugal at the time it made sense to approach King John II of Portugal, which he did in 1484. The king submitted his plan to a maritime committee which rejected it on technical grounds. The committee felt Columbus had significantly underestimated the ocean distance to Asia. Columbus based much of his view of world geography on a book called *Imago Mundi*, or "Image of the World," by a Frenchman named Pierre d'Ailly. According to d'Ailly, the Atlantic Ocean, or the Ocean Sea as it was called then, could be crossed in a few days with the aid of favorable winds. Apparently, Columbus was a believer for he left a margin note in his copy of *Imago Mundi*, "Between the edge of Spain and the beginning of India, the sea is short and can be crossed in a matter of a few days." His belief in the plan was evidently strengthened by correspondence with a distinguished Florentine physician and cosmographer Paolo Toscanelli, who had long advocated the feasibility of a western route to Asia. Paolo informed Columbus of a "sovereign known as the Grand Khan, a name which in our tongue"–Italian–"Means king of kings." The physician told of "Cipango," Marco Polo's name for Japan, where, "This island is most rich in gold and pearls and precious stones, and you should know that the temples and royal places are covered in solid gold."

The Portuguese authorities thought his estimate of the distance to Asia was much too small and that the voyage would not be possible. Much of King John's disinterest in Columbus's plan was because the Portuguese were already heavily invested in a search for an African route to India. The Portuguese explorer Bartolomeu Dias had successfully sailed around the southern tip of Africa, which fostered the belief of a potential eastern trade route to Asia. Hence, the king found Columbus's plan too risky and likely to fail.

Disheartened but not giving up, the explorer traveled to his home city of Genoa and Venice seeking support but found none. Columbus sent this brother Bartholomew to England to the court of King Henry VII to inquire if the English crown might sponsor such an expedition; the request was turned down. In France, Bartholomew approached King Charles VIII with the same plan, and met with the same disappointing results.

Chapter 2 – Columbus Appeals to King Ferdinand and Queen Isabella

"I see that the world is not so large as the vulgar opinion thinks it is." – Christopher Columbus

Columbus and his young son Diego traveled to Spain, where he intended to present his plan to Spanish sovereigns Ferdinand and Isabella. Through an acquaintance, Columbus was able to secure an audience with King Ferdinand and Queen Isabella. After listening to Columbus's plan for exploration, the sovereigns submitted his project to a commission headed by the Queen's confessor, Hernando de Talavera, for further investigation. While waiting for the decision of the committee, Columbus and Diego lived in Córdoba, Spain. The Monarchs were not interested in his plan at the time as the war in the south with the Muslims tied up their time and resources; however, they did give Columbus a yearly allowance and a letter ordering all cities within their kingdoms to provide the would-be explorer free food and lodging. After the death of his first wife, Columbus became involved with a young woman, Beatriz Enríquez de Harana, who bore a son they named Ferdinand. The boy would turn out to be a scholarly young man and go on to write a biography of his father that has become an invaluable source of information on the adventures of Columbus.

The main concern of the Talavera commission was how far Asia was from Europe if one sailed west. The commission came back with an unfavorable ruling for the same reason he had been rejected before--the distance to Asia was just too far for the small ships. To keep their options open, the king and queen kept him on the royal payroll while waiting for a more opportune time for his voyage. Columbus's opportunity came in January 1492 when, after nearly eight centuries, religious warfare between Spanish Christians and Moorish Muslims on the Iberian Peninsula came to an end. King Ferdinand and Queen Isabella won a decisive victory in a battle at the southern Spanish city of Granada, the last Muslim stronghold. Muslims were given a grave ultimatum: either be baptized into the Christian faith or be exiled.

Once again Columbus was granted an audience with the queen, who turned him down on the advice of her confessor. The discouraged explorer left for France to seek sponsorship. The royal advisors to Ferdinand and Isabella convinced them that if by some remote chance Columbus did succeed, then Spain would miss out on the discovery of the new lands and their potential riches. The advisor's recommendation was to let the explorer risk his own life in quest of "the grandeurs and secrets of the Universe" for the glory of Spain. The Catholic monarchs had just completed an expensive war in the Iberian Peninsula with the Moors and were wanting to gain an advantage in trade with Asia over the rival nations of Europe. Though Columbus's plan had little chance for success, it held the promise of offering Spain a competitive advantage. Ferdinand and Isabella decided to take a chance on Columbus and dispatched a messenger, who found him on the road and brought him back to the royal court. The king and queen agreed to his terms, giving him the hereditary title of "Admiral of the Ocean Sea, Viceroy, and Governor" and the rights to a tenth of the riches that came about from his voyage. In addition, he would have the right of buying one-eighth interest in any commercial venture that resulted from his discovery and receive one-eighth of the profits.

Figure – Painting "Columbus Before the Queen"
by Emanuel Gottlieb Leutze 1843.

Preparations for the Voyage

The Spanish court provided two ships for the expedition while Columbus raised the funds for a third. The small caravel, the *Niña*, was commanded by Vicente Pinzón, and a similar ship, the *Pinta*, was commanded by Vicente's brother, Martín Pinzón. The third and larger ship was the *Santa María*, which was captained by Columbus. The two smaller ships or caravels, the *Niña* and *Pinta*, were the type used by Portuguese traders that worked along the coast of Europe and Asia. The exact specifications of the ships are not known, but they were believed to be about 60 tons of capacity and about 50 feet long. The small ships had three sails, could sail in shallow water, and had a crew of about twenty-five. The caravels were single-decked with a minimum of superstructure and cabin accommodations. The flagship of the fleet was the larger *Santa Maria*, a merchant class ship of about 125 tons of capacity and about 65 feet long. This larger ship could carry more men and cargo than the smaller caravels but was less maneuverable and drafted more water. The exact dimensions of the three ships are unknown and are now the subject of educated guesses.

THE FLEET OF COLUMBUS.

Figure – The fleet of Columbus's three ships.

The crews for the three ships totaled ninety able seamen recruited from the seafaring community in local towns and villages. They stocked the ships with salted cod, bacon, biscuits, wine, olive oil, and enough water for a year. To navigate his ships, Columbus and the two Pinzón brothers employed the technology of the day: hourglasses to measure time, a compass for direction, a chip log to measure speed, and an astrolabe used to calculate latitude. To determine the distance traveled each day, they estimated their speed through the water and multiplied by the time under sail, a technique known as dead reckoning.

Chapter 3 -
Setting Sail for the New World

"This night of October 11-12 was one big with destiny for the human race, the most momentous ever experienced aboard any ship in any sea." -- Samuel Eliot Morison, Author of Admiral of the Ocean Sea

The three ships bound for points unknown set sail on the morning of September 3, 1492, from the small Spanish port city Palos. The ships sailed first to the Canary Islands, off the west coast of Africa, to take advantage of their southerly latitude, which Columbus believed was the same as Japan. Also, the easterly trade winds prevailed in the latitude, which would carry them to the west. On September 6, after taking on fresh supplies and making a few repairs in the Canaries, the fleet weighed anchor. The tradewinds pushed them steadily westward through calm seas, sailing west under a fair wind. Their latitude was the most northerly for which, in late summer, the northeast trade wind could be expected. The winds at that latitude proved to be somewhat unreliable and later voyages were further south for steadier winds to power their sails. By the end of September, the crews began to grow restless, "scaring themselves with...the idea that since the wind was always at their backs, they would never have a wind in those waters for returning to Spain." Columbus calmed his crew, and they continued to sail westerly with no land in sight.

Sailors of that period normally sailed not far from a known coastline and were unaccustomed to sailing for weeks in the open ocean with no reliable maps to guide them. The Atlantic Ocean, or "Ocean Sea" as it was then known, was a forbidding place, believed to be full of monsters lurking beneath the surface. Legends told of giant sea serpents that could rise from the deep and crush a small ship with a single blow. For those who still believed the earth was flat, they feared falling off the edge of the world and plunging into the fiery abyss of the setting sun. This world of wind, wave, and unknown creatures was no place for the timid; rather, it was a realm that only the very brave or foolish men dared to venture. To add an element of apprehension for the crew, Columbus was an Italian--a foreigner--not to be trusted by the hardened Spanish sailors under his command.

As the days passed, signs of land started to appear—birds and pieces of wood in the sea—and they became more frequent, which did much to calm the fears of the crew and prevent a mutiny. Columbus feared that if land were not found soon, his crew would simply throw him overboard and return to Spain. The next day a flock of birds was spotted flying southwest–a sign that land was near. Columbus ordered the ships to follow the birds. The next night, the moon rose in the east around midnight, illuminating the night sky. Two hours later Rodrigo de Triana, aboard the Pinta, spotted a strip of beach in the distance and excitedly shouted, "land, land." The captain of the Pinta, Martín Pinzón, quickly verified the sighting of land and fired a cannon to signal the other two ships of the fateful discovery.

Figure – Replica of Columbus's ship the Niña built in 1991.

Land at Last

As the light of day filled the morning sky of October 12, the fleet of three ships dropped anchor in the calm emerald blue water and went ashore to be greeted by a party of partially naked natives. The island, only 13 miles long and 6 miles wide, was called Guanahani by the natives, which is believed to be San Salvador (formerly Watling Island) in the Bahamas today. Columbus assumed he had landed on one of the islands discovered by Marco Polo on his exploration of Asia, which he named San Salvador or "Holy Savior." Columbus and his men offered gifts of hawk's bells, used to track birds in falconry, and glass beads to the natives. In return, the brown-skinned natives presented the visitors with squawking parrots and skeins of cotton thread. To validate his discovery, Columbus summoned the fleet's secretary to "witness that I was taking possession of this island for King and Queen." Since Columbus believed he had landed in Asia, he called the local inhabitants "Indians." The Indians were of the Taínos tribe and generally friendly to Columbus and his men. To Columbus the natives were "artless and generous with what they have, to such a degree as no one would believe but he who had seen it. Of anything they have, if it be asked for, they never say no, but do rather invite the person to accept it, and show as much lovingness as though they would give their hearts." The next day, crowds of Indians appeared on the beach to watch the three ships at anchor. Others approached the ships in dugout canoes bringing gifts that Columbus described as "trifles too tedious to describe." The visitors were not interested in the modest gifts; rather, it was gold that they sought. Small amounts of gold were spotted in the natives' jewelry, which piqued the men's interest. Columbus assumed the gold was from the island of Cipango–Japan. To guide the fleet to Japan and China and to act as translators, Columbus had six of the natives kidnapped. He later wrote, "In the first island that I found, I took some of them [Indians] by force, to the intent that they should learn and give me information of what there was in those parts."

The Taínos were both horticulturalists and expert navigators. The natives had been in the region for thousands of years and had developed a complex agricultural and trading society. Each of the villages was governed by a local chief, known as a caciques, who answered to a paramount chief named Guacanagari, a man that would become known to Columbus. He and the other chiefs presided over a trading network that was the lifeblood of the people on the islands. The natives had large ocean-going canoes that could carry up to 150 men, which allowed travel to distant mainland villages in Florida and Mesoamerica. They traded in feathers, gold, wood, pottery, cotton fabric, and food stuffs.

Figure – Painting "Landing of Columbus" by John Vanderlyn, 1847. The scene depicts Columbus raising the royal banner, claiming the land for his Spanish patrons, standing with his hat at his feet in honor of the sacredness of the event. The crew displays a variety of emotions with some searching for gold on the beach. The natives of the island watch cautiously from behind a tree.

Without a clear plan, the three ships explored the Bahama island chain with captain and crew captivated by the beauty of this strange new world. The admiral wrote, "I discovered a very wonderful harbor with one mouth, or rather one might say two mouths, for it has an island in the middle, and both are very narrow, and within it is wide enough for 100 ships, if it were deep and clean." The landscape, flora, and trees were so different than anything he had seen in Europe, recording, "During this time I walked around some trees which were the most beautiful thing that I had ever seen, viewed as much verdure in so great development as in the month of May in Andalusia, and all the trees were so different from ours as day from night." The enormity of his discovery was becoming clear to the explorer: This new land of different vegetation and people would take a lifetime to explore and map, yet he was due back in Spain within six months.

Cuba and the Discovery of Tobacco

Columbus believed they were near Japan and China and continued his search of the nearby islands looking for gold and the riches of the Orient. The fleet sailed along the southern coast of what is today Cuba. Columbus found Cuba an enchanting place, writing "the most beautiful that eyes have ever seen: full of very good harbors and deep rivers." The natives told him of ten great rivers and that the land was so large that it could not be circumnavigated in 20 days in their canoes. Thinking it was the coast of China, he sent emissaries to visit the Great Khan or emperor of China. The shore party failed to find any Chinese, Arabs, descendants of the Lost Tribes of Israel, or the Great Khan, but they did observe "many people who carried a firebrand to light certain herbs the smoke of which they inhale." The Europeans had just had their first encounter with tobacco, which would grow into a large industry in the centuries to come. The islanders lived on rudimentary agriculture, fishing, and gathering mollusks. They wore few clothes, but possessed small quantities of gold from gravel collected in streams and fashioned it into jewelry. The Spaniards bartered vigorously with the natives to obtain their gold.

From Cuba the fleet crossed the Windward Passage and sailed along the north coast of a large island Columbus called "Hispaniola," which is today Haiti and the Dominican Republic. There, in the middle of the night, the *Santa Maria* ran aground. Trouble started late Christmas Eve when the admiral "decided to stretch out and sleep." The exhausted Columbus turned over the helm to one of the seamen, who gave the helm to another; finally, the duty of steering the *Santa Maria* fell to a fourteen or fifteen-year-old ship's boy. Though the sea was calm, and the wind was light, the inexperienced young lad allowed the ship to drift onto a sandy reef. The ship was torn apart by the constant crashing of the waves against the hull, smashing it against the rocky shore. Columbus was forced to abandon the ship and with the help of the friendly Indian chief Guacanagarí and his people, the crew and most of the supplies were saved. Since the fleet was now short their largest ship, Columbus was forced to leave 39 of the men behind to live off the land until a return voyage could be arranged. With the warm climate, friendly native women, and their thirst for gold, he had no trouble finding men willing to stay behind. The fortress was called "La Navidad" by Columbus.

Aboard the *Niña*, the admiral departed the island but left the fort well stocked with provisions to keep the men alive until he could return to rescue the stranded men.

Before returning to Spain in mid-January 1493, Columbus made his last stop in the New World at Samaná Peninsula on the northeastern coast of Hispaniola. There they encountered the warrior-like Cigüayos tribe, and a skirmish broke out between the Spaniards and the natives over trade for bows and arrows, resulting in one Indian being stabbed and another with an arrow wound to the chest. Because of the encounter with the Indians, Columbus named the inlet the "Bay of Arrows." Additional natives were taken captive for the long journey back to Spain.

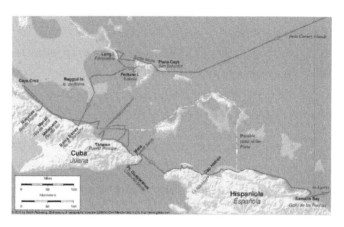

Figure - Map of the first voyage
of Christopher Columbus, 1492-1493.

A Triumphant Return to Spain

The *Niña* and *Pinta* sailed northeast from Hispaniola until they encountered a westerly trade wind that pushed them toward home. The route that Columbus had navigated, a southerly route from Europe to the New World and a northerly return route home would become a standard route for generations of sailors to come. The ships encountered heavy storms and became separated. The storm was so severe that "...the admiral and all the people made a vow that, upon reaching the first land, they would all go in their shirts in procession to make a prayer in a church that was dedicated to Our Lady. Beside the general or common vows, everyone made his special vow, because nobody expected to escape, holding themselves all for lost, owing to the terrible tempest that they were experiencing." The storm forced the *Niña* into port at the island of Santa Maria in the Azores. Many of the crew went ashore to a local church to say their prayers of thanksgiving for surviving the storm. While praying the men were imprisoned by the island's captain, fearing they were pirates. After a two-day standoff, the prisoners were released, allowing Columbus and his crew to set sail for Spain.

As they were approaching the coast of Spain, they were blown off course by a fierce storm that drove the *Niña* into port at Lisbon. The *Niña* arrived at the harbor in Lisbon and Columbus eventually located King John for a meeting. Due to the poor relationships between Spain and Portugal, the meeting didn't go well, and the king claimed the voyage was in violation of the 1479 Treaty of Alcácovas. Columbus feared arrest but was released to travel to Spain. On March 15, 1493, the *Niña* arrived in the port of Palos, with the *Pinta* arriving later that same day. Columbus, his men, and several captive Indians were received with much fanfare by the Spanish Court. The Spanish royalty was expecting the explorer's return as Columbus had sent word to the king and queen from Lisbon announcing their successful voyage and subsequent return. In Barcelona Columbus met with the Spanish king and queen to receive well-deserved praise and their highest honors. This was truly the hour of Columbus's crowning glory. Soon plans were made for a second trip to the new world to retrieve his men and seek further conquest.

Figure – Painting "The return of Christopher Columbus; his audience before King Ferdinand and Queen Isabella," by the French painter Eugène Delacroix in 1839.

On the advice of Columbus, Ferdinand and Isabella sought support from the Pope to counter Portugal's claim to the discoveries of Columbus. Pope Alexander VI, himself a Spaniard, issued a series of bulls (decrees) in favor of the Spanish claims to the new lands. The most important of the bulls, *Inter Caetera*, divided the Atlantic into eastern and western areas of exploration, with Spain being allotted the western area. This principle of demarcation of areas was accepted by the Portuguese government in the Treaty of Tordesillas in 1494.

The first journey to the New World was a voyage of discovery; the next two were voyages of conquest and colonization. This is where the image of Columbus takes a dark turn. Christopher Columbus would turn out to be a much better explorer than governor of a new continent.

Chapter 4 -
The Second Voyage

"All great men make mistakes." – Winston Churchill

The excitement brought about by the success of the first voyage allowed Columbus to assemble a large fleet of seventeen ships for the second voyage. On board were over a thousand men destined to colonize the new and abundant land to the west. The ships were laden with seeds, plants, tools, livestock, and many other items needed to establish a trading outpost. Those on board consisted of a society in miniature: priests, gentleman-soldiers, farmers, and artisans. The only thing lacking was enough food for the first year. They had stocked the ships optimistic of their ability to live off the land. The purpose of the new colony was to settle the island of Hispaniola, found a farming and mining community that was self-sufficient, and return gold and treasure back to Spain. The settlement was also to serve as a base to search for a route to China and India. The fleet departed from Cádiz in early September and reached the island of Dominica in the Lesser Antilles on November 3, 1493. The ships meandered through the island chain, reaching

Hispaniola in the middle of November. Columbus was shocked to learn that the men he had left behind at La Navidad had been killed and their fort destroyed.

The Indian chief Guacanagarí told Columbus of the fate of the Spaniards. According to the chief, as soon as Columbus had left the island the men began to quarrel amongst themselves. Searching for gold, food, and women they invaded the country of another powerful cacique named Caonabó, who became provoked and slayed them and destroyed their encampment. The cacique was wise in his method of attack on the Spaniards; rather than a straightforward frontal attack, he picked them off one by one until the braves could overwhelm the intruders and destroy them. Guacanagarí and his men attempted in vain to defend the Spaniards, even showing Columbus the wound he had received in the battle. Columbus's men wanted to kill the chief, but the admiral believed his story and sailed further east along the Hispaniola coast and founded the town of La Isabella, named after the Queen. The site for La Isabella turned out to be a poor one, with a harbor that lacked abundant fish and fresh water over a mile away--the colony never prospered. Columbus left his brother Diego in charge of the island then sailed with three ships "to explore the mainland of the Indies."

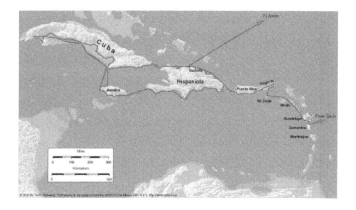

Figure – Map of the second voyage of Columbus, 1493 -1496.

Still believing Cuba was a part of Asia, he sailed down the southern coast of Cuba hoping to reach Japan. Next he sailed south to discover the island of Jamaica, finding it inhabited by Indians that had a similar language and culture as the Taínos they had encountered on Cuba and Hispaniola, but were more warlike. In early May 1494, the Columbian fleet approached St. Ann's' Bay on the northern shore of Jamaica and were greeted by sixty or seventy canoes full of shouting warriors. To scatter the natives, the ship's cannons fired blank salvos.

In June 1494 he sailed back to Hispaniola to find the island in revolt. His brother Diego had proven to be a poor governor and was unable to control the Spanish settlers. Though suffering from painful arthritis that had kept him bedridden for weeks, Columbus took over the presidency of the governing council and endeavored to bring order to the chaos. Things had gotten way out of hand as gangs of soldiers and discontented colonists ravaged the island, terrorizing the natives and committing every sort of brutality. The admiral, believing that Christians could do no wrong, held the Indians responsible for the misdeeds rather than the colonists. Using horses and hounds, the colonists rounded up over fifteen hundred of the natives and brought them to Isabella. About five hundred, "the best males and females," were loaded on ships for the slave market of Seville. Then Columbus allowed the Christians to pick from the remainder for personal use. Some four hundred were left and were told to leave. Fearing recapture, the desperate Indians fled with such haste that some of the mothers left their babies on the ground and ran for their lives. The fate of the Indians aboard the slave ship was dismal. Unaccustomed to life at sea, nearly half died before they reached Spain.

To defend themselves against the Spanish, the Taínos of Hispaniola banded together to drive the Spaniards into the sea. The cacique Guatiguaná attempted to unite the tribes on the island to defeat the much smaller number of Spanish invaders. In a scenario that would play out repeatedly in the coming centuries, the natives failed to unite against the Europeans, thus greatly weakening their resistance. Columbus, who had now regained his strength, marched out of Isabella to meet the large band of Indians with a force of two hundred men, twenty horses, and twenty Spanish war dogs. The experienced Spanish soldiers made quick work of the inexperienced native combatants. The Indians, "who imagined that man and horse were one animal," were devastated, resulting in another large group of slaves gathered up by the conquering Spanish.

Word had reached the sovereigns of the brutal treatment of the natives. The admiral sailed for Spain in March 1496 to defend himself and his brothers in court against charges from the colonists of his mis-governance and cruelty. He was received by the sovereigns pleasantly but with none of the fanfare of the first voyage. Many of the slaves from Hispaniola died during the passage and the remainder were released by the queen's order and sent back home. It was becoming clear to all but Columbus that the Indies was not a land of great wealth there for the taking. The colonists began to search for a better location for the capitol of Hispaniola as La Isabella had proven unsuitable. An exploration party was sent out and selected a site on the southeastern coast of the island. The site of the future city of Santa Domingo offered a good harbor, fertile land for agriculture, and gold bearing rivers that had not been worked. By late 1496 or early 1497 the building of Santo Domingo had commenced. La Isabella was abandoned, and Santo Domingo became the first permanent European city in the New World. Bartholomew Columbus became the new settlement's leader.

Chapter 5 -
The Third Voyage

"The land which God has newly given your Highnesses on this voyage much be reckoned continental in extent."
– Christopher Columbus, letter to Ferdinand and Isabella, October 1498

Word had spread among the Spaniards about the harsh living conditions in the western colony, making it hard for Columbus to recruit colonists for the third voyage. To provide colonists, the sovereigns pardoned certain minor criminals who agreed to stay in the Indies for one to two years; in addition, this was the first voyage that allowed women to travel to the New World. With six ships, Columbus left Spain in late May 1498. The fleet divided into two groups, with three of the ships going directly to the colony at Hispaniola carrying much needed supplies, while Columbus took the other three ships on a voyage of exploration. Columbus's fleet took a southerly route in the belief that gold and precious stones could be found in the "hot" zone. The fleet reached the island of Trinidad, off the coast of Venezuela, on July 31. He sailed through the channel he named the Serpent's Mouth and crossed the Gulf of Paria to the coast of Venezuela. On August 5, 1498, his men went ashore but Columbus stayed aboard the ship with a serious eye infection, which was the first recorded landing by Europeans on the American continent. In the bay of Paria, Columbus and his men observed vast quantities of fresh water pouring from the delta of the Orinoco River. This large volume of fresh water could not be produced by a mere island; rather, it indicated a significant land mass. Columbus recorded in his journal: "I believe that this is a very great continent, until today unknown." In his mind this was no ordinary place but rather the Biblical Garden of Eden.

After further investigation of the coast of Venezuela, Columbus set sail for Hispaniola to the new settlement his brother had founded. The exhausted Columbus found the colony near rebellion. The settlers had already traded for all the gold held by the native islanders and had driven the natives to the point of war with their constant demands for gold, food, and women. Many of the settlers were in open revolt against Bartholomew's authority, claiming they had been misled about the riches of the New World. To calm the settlers, Columbus bought off the angry settlers with pardons, restoration of their offices, and land grants. In addition, the "Indians" were given to the settlers as domestic servants, laborers, and mine workers. For a time, the rebels were quieted but the damage had been done to Columbus' reputation as a governor.

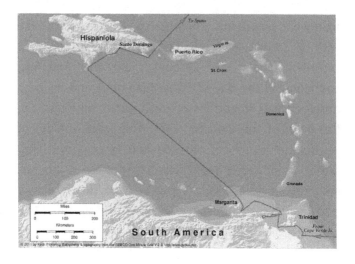

Figure - Map of the third voyage
of Christopher Columbus, 1498-1500.

To relieve the admiral of his many burdens as a governor, in October 1499 he sent two ships to Spain asking for the Court of Spain to appoint a royal commissioner to aid him in the governance of the island. The sovereigns sent Francisco de Bobadilla to take over control of the island and investigate the complaints against the admiral. Bobadilla arrived in Santo Domingo while Columbus was away on his third voyage. The settlers confronted Bobadilla with a storm of complaints against Columbus and his two brothers Bartholomew and Diego. The three brothers were accused of using brutal and extreme measures of torture and mutilation to govern Hispaniola. As a result of the reports of the heinous actions, Bobadilla sent

Columbus and his two brothers back to Spain in chains. After six weeks of imprisonment in Spain the men were released, and the king and queen restored them with their titles and revenues. However, Christopher was stripped of his authority and never again was allowed to exercise his authority as admiral and viceroy or to intervene in the government of the Indies.

Chapter 6 -
The Final Voyage

"God made me the messenger of the new heaven and the new earth of which he spoke in the Apocalypse of St. John, after having spoken of it through the mouth of Isaiah, and he showed me the spot where to find it."
Christopher Columbus, letter to Juana de La Torre, 1500

For his next voyage, which would be his last, he had trouble securing financial backing and permission. Permission was granted providing Columbus would stay away from Hispaniola, where a new governor, Nicolás de Ovando, had been appointed. The goal of this final voyage, or the "high voyage" as the admiral called it, was to find the strait that led to the Indian Ocean, thus opening a sea path to China and the Orient. The fleet of four caravels set sail in mid-May 1502, reaching Martinique twenty-one days later. Accompanying the 51-year-old admiral, who was failing in health, was his 13-year-old son Fernando, his brother Bartholomew, and many of his old friends and shipmates from previous voyages. Columbus had been forbidden to land at Hispaniola by the sovereigns; however, he had to defy their authority to replace a leaking ship. Due to the many sea voyages his ships had become infested with seaworms that bored into the wooden hull and over time caused leaks that would ultimately sink a ship.

Against the sovereigns' wishes, Columbus approached Santo Domingo, but governor Ovando refused to let him land or anchor. Columbus was seeking a safe harbor for what he believed was a hurricane that was approaching. His four ships found a safe harbor in southern Hispaniola to ride out the storm. Ovando did not heed the admiral's warning of the impending storm and allowed a fleet of 30 ships to return to Spain, only two of which arrived in Spain. The loss of the fleet in the hurricane resulted in some 500 deaths, including the governor Francisco de Bobadilla, and a large cargo of gold which plunged into the ocean's depths. Ferdinand Columbus wrote of the storm, "This is why the admiral's enemies charged that by his magic arts he had raised that storm to take revenge on Bobadilla and others of his enemies who were with him." To Columbus's great luck, one of the ships that did survive the hurricane was carrying his personal gold, which he was able to retrieve when he returned to Spain.

His fleet sailed west along the shore of Jamaica, next crossing the Caribbean to the Bay Islands off the coast of Honduras. Unable to find the strait to the Indian Ocean, he traveled down the Caribbean coasts of Honduras, Nicaragua, and Costa Rica. At Almirante Bay, in present day Republic of Panama, Columbus learned from the natives that he was on an isthmus between two great seas. Little did he realize that he was only fifty miles by land from the Pacific Ocean, hence the elusive route to the Orient. Giving up hope on finding a water passage to the Indian Ocean, he now focused his attention on the search for gold. They did find gold in what is modern day Panama, prompting him to build a settlement there where Columbus left his brother Bartholomew in charge. At first the local Indians were friendly but once they realized the Spaniards were building a permanent colony, they became hostile. After attacks by the Indians, Columbus was forced to abandon the settlement, taking the survivors to Hispaniola.

The problem of the seaworms destroying his ships was becoming acute and Columbus was forced to abandon one of his ships. Before they could return to Hispaniola, another ship had to be abandoned. With two ships remaining, both of which had water almost up to their decks, the worm eaten ships were run aground on the north coast of Jamaica. Being marooned on the island of Jamaica, Columbus sent two men in a dug-out canoe with natives as the rowing crew to bring help from the colony at Hispaniola. After a failed attempt, the men finally reached Hispaniola safely, but Governor Ovando was hostile toward Columbus and in no hurry to send help. A year later, in 1504, a rescue ship was sent to Jamaica to retrieve Columbus and his men.

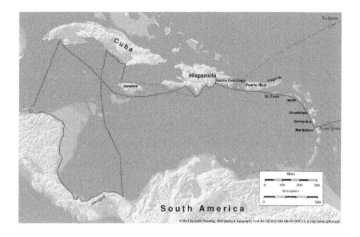

Figure – Map of the fourth and final voyage
of Christopher Columbus, 1502-1504.

Final Days

Columbus returned to Spain with his brother and son in November 1504. When he arrived, he learned that Queen Isabella was on her deathbed. The fourth voyage had been a success, as he brought back valuable information about the previously unexplored coasts of Central and South America and a substantial amount of gold. The king waited until the spring of 1505 to allow the admiral an audience. The shrewd monarch had no intention of granting the explorer the enormous political and economic rights he claimed were due him. Columbus passed the last year of his life in relative obscurity seeking from the royal court the privileges and wealth he had been promised.

The hard life at sea started to take its toll on his body by the winter of 1504-1505. By 1505 he spent many days in bed suffering from a debilitating and painful arthritis. On May 20, 1506, his condition grew much worse. A priest was called to his bed to administer last rites. At his death bed were his two sons, Don Diego and Ferdinand; some of the loyal men who had been with him at sea; and a few faithful domestics. After the priest's final prayer, the dying admiral was heard to say in a faint voice the final words of his Lord and Savior as he was dying on the cross, *in manus tuas, Domine, commendo, spiritum meum*, or "Father, into your hands I commit my spirit." And with this, the admiral of the Ocean Sea, discoverer of worlds, passed into immortality.

Based on what sketchy historical evidence there is on the health of Columbus, medical historians believe he died from Reiter's Syndrome. His symptoms during his final years of his life were consistent with the presentation of the disease, which is a reactive arthritis, a joint inflammation caused by intestinal bacterial infections. The disease was probably acquired during one of his ocean voyages because of the poor sanitation and lack of proper food preparation techniques.

Columbus's hereditary titles of admiral and viceroy went to his son Diego, who remained in good standing with the royal court and was made governor of Hispaniola three years later. The younger son, who was not a legitimate heir, inherited his father's books.

Chapter 7 - Legacy of Columbus and Spanish Colonization

"An old man, broken with the storms of state is come to lay his weary bones among ye; give him a little earth for charity." -- William Shakespeare, Henry VIII

No man since Augustus Caesar had done more to directly impact the course of human history than Christopher Columbus. Yet many of his personal goals were unfulfilled at his death; he had not found the strait to the Indian Ocean, or met the Great Khan, or converted many savages to Christianity, nor had he secured the future for his family. At his death, the vast potential of the Americas was only dimly seen, and it would take generations to explore and subdue this vast land. The Americas would eventually have been discovered, probably by accident, even if the Enterprise of the Indies had never happened. Through his vision, determination, and tenacity, his grand plan of discovery came to fruition. A product of his time and flawed in many ways, he was a bold visionary who profoundly changed the course of human history.

As word spread quickly throughout Europe of Columbus's discoveries, others began their own voyages to the New World. Though Christopher Columbus is generally credited with the discovery of North and South America, he did not coin the name "America." That distinction goes to a Florentine businessman and explorer named Amerigo Vespucci. Between 1497 and 1504, Vespucci led expeditions that mapped parts of the eastern coasts of North and South America, publishing his results widely in Europe. He claimed that Brazil was part of a different continent, not part of Asia as Columbus asserted. Vespucci's claims inspired the cartographer Martin Waldseemüller to recognize Vespucci's accomplishment by placing the name "America" on a map of the New World. Other map makers followed suit and by 1532 the name America was firmly associated with two new continents.

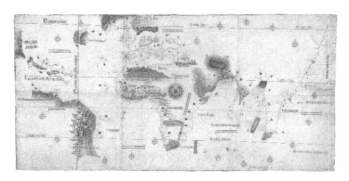

Figure – The Cantino World Map of 1502, the earliest surviving map of Portuguese and Columbus discoveries. The West Indies and the coast of Brazil are on the left of the map. The line on the left shows the Papal demarcation of territory – Spain to the west, Portugal to the east – according to the Treaty of Tordesillas.

The Spanish rapidly began to colonize the New World, establishing colonies in Hispaniola, Cuba, Puerto Rico, Jamaica, and the other smaller islands. To work the gold mines and ranches, the natives were put to work in hellish conditions. Those who resisted were either killed, sometimes very brutally, or shipped back to Spain as slaves. The Catholic Priest Bartolomé de las Casas, who witnessed firsthand much of the cruelty inflected upon the natives, wrote, "I have seen the greatest cruelty and inhumanity practiced on these gentle and peace-loving [native peoples]...without any reason except for insatiable greed, thirst, and hunger for gold."

With the European colonization of the New World came diseases, such as smallpox, measles, and other deadly diseases to which the natives had no natural immunity. As a result, the native population began a dramatic decline. The once plentiful Tíano Indians who had greeted Columbus as he set foot in the New World ceased to exist as a distinct race of people within fifty years. With the native population in decline, black slaves from Africa were imported to work the ranches and sugar cane fields. Though Christopher Columbus was not the first European to set foot in the New World, his voyages were significant in that they opened the door for further exploration and colonization–for good or ill.

The End

Thank you for purchasing this book. I hope you enjoyed reading it. Please don't forget to leave a review of the book. I read each one, and they help me become a better writer.

- Doug

Christopher Columbus Timeline

1451 – Born in the port city of Genoa (Italy) the son of a prosperous wool merchant and tavern keeper.

1476 – Swims ashore to Portugal after his ship is sunk in a battle with pirates. His brother Bartholomew joins him in Lisbon.

1477 to 1484 – Travels as a merchant mariner on voyages from Iceland to Guinea.

1479 – Marries Felipa Moniz Perestrello the daughter of a wealthy Portuguese nobleman and they settle on the island of Porto Santo, near Madeira.

1479 or 1480 – First son Diego is born.

1484 – Conceives of "The Enterprise of the Indies" idea but fails to convince the king of Portugal, King John II, to fund the plan. Wife Felipa dies.

1485 – Moves to Palos, Spain.

1488 – Second son Fernando is born to Beatriz Enriquez de Harana at Cordova, Spain.

September 3, 1492 – Departs from Palos, sails to Canary Island to repair and refit fleet of three ships.

October 12, 1492 – Land is sighted in New World at 2:00 a.m. by Rodrigo de Triana. Names island San Salvador.

October 29, 1492 – Arrives in Cuba.

November 22, 1492 – Captain of the *Pinta*, Martín Alonso Pinzón, deserts the expedition to search for gold on an island called "Babeque" by the natives.

December 5, 1492 – Arrives at the island he names Hispaniola.

December 25, 1492 – *Santa Maria* runs aground on Hispaniola, founds a settlement he calls La Navidad.

January 6, 1493 – Pinzón rejoins Columbus.

January 16, 1493 – Departs Hispaniola for Spain aboard the *Niña*.

February 14, 1493 – Niña and Pinta are separated during a storm.

February 15, 1493 – Lands on Santa Maria Island in the Azores.

March 4, 1493 – Blown off course by a storm, the *Niña* goes into port at Lisbon, Portugal.

March 15, 1493 – *Niña* and Pinta arrive separately in Palos, Spain.

September 1493 – Fleet of 17 ships depart from Cádiz, Spain, for Columbus's second voyage.

November 3, 1493 – Island of Dominica sighted at dawn.

November 22, 1493 – Lands at Hispaniola.

November 28, 1493 – Returns to La Navidad to find the fort destroyed and the men killed or missing.

December 1493 – Founds colony of La Isabella on the island of Hispaniola in the present day Dominican Republic.

April 24, 1494 – Sails from La Isabella in search for the mainland Japan.

April 30, 1494 – Lands in Cuba.

June 13, 1494 – Returns to Hispaniola.

August 20, 1494 – Returns to La Isabella and becomes the governor.

1494 – 1495 – Spaniards and Taíno Indians at war.

March 10, 1496 – Sails for Spain.

June 8, 1496 – Reaches the coast of Portugal.

May 30, 1498 – Departs form Sanlucar, Spain, with six ships for third voyage to the Indies.

June 19, 1498 – Arrives in the Canary Islands; splits fleet into two squadrons, one bound for Hispaniola, while Columbus takes three ships on a more southernly route.

July 31, 1498 – Arrives at Trinidad.

August 13, 1498 – Leaves the Gulf of Paria.

August 19, 1498 – Arrives at Santo Domingo on Hispaniola and resumes his role as governor.

October 1500 – Arrested along with his two brothers and sent back to Spain in chains.

May 11, 1502 – Departs from Cádiz, Spain, with four ships for last voyage to the Indies.

June 29, 1502 – Arrives at Santo Domingo, Hispaniola.

June 25, 1503 – Marooned along with crew in Jamaica.

June 29, 1504 – Rescued from Jamaica after more than a year on the island.

November 7, 1504 – Returns to Spain.

November 12, 1504 – Queen Isabella I of Castile dies.

May 20, 1506 – Dies at Valladolid, Spain.

Biographical Sketches

<u>Columbus, Bartholomew</u> (c. 1461 - 1514) was an Italian navigator, public official, and brother of Christopher Columbus. Bartholomew Columbus was born in Genoa, Italy, and probably lived in Lisbon, Portugal, in 1477, working as a map maker and mariner. His brother Christopher sent him to England in 1488 to solicit funds from King Henry VII for a voyage of discovery. Failing in England, he went to France and was turned down by King Charles VIII. He was in Fontainebleau, France, when his brother landed on the island of San Salvador in 1492.

In 1493 Bartholomew returned to Spain and Queen Isabella put him in charge of three supply ships bound for Hispaniola. His brother, Diego, was already there as he had traveled on his brother Christopher's second voyage. Bartholomew became the lieutenant governor of the Indies and administrator of Hispaniola from 1496 to 1498. Troubles on the island with rebellious settlers forced the sovereigns to remove Bartholomew and replace him with Francisco de Bobadilla in 1500. Along with his brothers Christopher and Diego, Bobadilla sent Bartholomew back to Spain in chains. Both were freed by the sovereigns and restored to their positions. He traveled again to the Indies on his brother's fourth voyage, and again with his nephew Diego in 1509.

<u>Columbus, Diego (also called Giacomo)</u> (1450? – 1515) was an Italian mariner and brother of Christopher Columbus. Diego Columbus was born in Genoa, Italy, and sailed on his brother's second voyage to the New World in 1493. His brother Christopher appointed Diego as governor of the settlement of La Isabella on the island of Hispaniola. He proved to be a poor administrator and the settlers broke out into a revolt. When Christopher returned to the island, he took back control of the settlements. Diego returned to Spain in 1500 and became a priest.

<u>Columbus, Diego</u> (c. 1480 – 1526) was the governor of Hispaniola and eldest son of Christopher Columbus and his wife Felipa Moniz Perestrello. Diego Columbus was probably born in Lisbon, Portugal, and received instruction at a monastery near Palos, Spain. From 1492 to 1506 he served as attendant to Prince Don Juan in the Spanish court. After his father's death he claimed his father's hereditary rights and honors, winning them after a long legal battle with King Ferdinand. Confirmed as admiral of the Indies in 1509, he sailed to the New World and became governor of Hispaniola until his recall in 1523.

<u>Columbus, Ferdinand</u> (1488 – 1539) was the youngest son and biographer of Christopher Columbus. Ferdinand Columbus was born in Cordova, Spain, to his father's

mistress Beatriz Enríquez de Harana. After his father returned from his first voyage to the New World, Fernando was appointed as a page to the Prince of Asturias but transferred his service to Queen Isabella I upon the death of the young prince. He accompanied his father on his fourth voyage to the New World and then sailed to Santo Domingo in 1509 with his half-brother Diego and stayed for six months. He received large grants from the Spanish crown, became wealthy, and collected some 20,000 books to form a library. The library also contained Christopher Columbus's books, which have personal annotations on the pages that have helped scholars understand the explorer's life. The remains of Ferdinand's library are maintained today at the Seville Cathedra.

Isabella I of Castile (1451 – 1504) (called Isabella the Catholic). Isabella was the daughter of John II of Castile and his second wife, Isabella of Portugal. She married Ferdinand II of Aragon in 1469. Upon the death of her brother she became the queen of Castile in 1474. This brought the kingdoms of Aragon and Castile under one rule. Although the two kingdoms were governed separately, public ordinances of the kingdoms were signed by both the king and queen. During their reign, numerous reforms were made in political and ecclesiastical matters, schools were established, and learning and the arts were developed. She brought the crime rate to the lowest level it had been in years and unburdened the kingdom of the large debt her brother had left behind. After a multi-year war with the Moorish Kingdom of Granada there on the Iberian Peninsula in 1492, the explorer Christopher Columbus gained a special patronage of Isabella. Columbus's voyages of discovery were successful, thus opening large territories in the New World for Spanish exploration and conquest. As a result, Spain became a major European power for over a century. Isabella was known for her intelligence, her broad political vision, and her high moral character.

Figure – The wedding portrait
of Ferdinand and Isabella, c. 1469.

King John II of Portugal (João II in Portuguese) (1455 – 1495) was the king of Portugal from 1481 until his death in 1495. John II was born in Lisbon to King Afonso V of Portugal and his wife Isabella of Coimbra. John II became ruler of Portugal in 1477 when his father retired and became king in 1481 after the death of his father. Upon taking the throne he instigated a series of measures to curtail the power of the aristocracy and concentrate power within the crown. John II was a proponent of voyages of discovery to enrich the crown. He sponsored exploration of the coast of Africa and funded Bartolomeu Dias's discovery of the passage of the Cape of Good Hope around the southern tip of Africa. The king failed to sponsor Christopher Columbus's voyage of discovery and came into conflict with the Spanish sovereigns over the legitimacy of the explorer's discoveries. With a papal mediator, Spain and Portugal negotiated the Treaty of Tordesillas in 1494, which divided all newly discovered lands in the New World between Spain and Portugal.

Figure - Supposed portrait of King John II of Portugal.

Notes on Dates and Names

The name *Christopher Columbus* is the anglicized version of the Latin Christophorus Columbus. The Italian form of Christopher Columbus's name is Cristoforo Colombo and the Spanish version is Cristóbal Colón. Dates are given in the Julian calendar, which had been in effect since 45 BC, and was the calendar Columbus used. To compensate for the accumulation of errors in the Julian calendar Pope Gregory XIII in 1583 initiated a new calendar, which is still used today. The new calendar added ten days, so October 5 became October 15.

References and Further Reading

Bergreen, Laurence. *Columbus: The Four Voyages*. Viking. 2011.

Boyle, David. *Toward the Setting Sun: Columbus, Cabot, Vespucci, and the Race for America*. Walker Publishing Company, Inc. 2008.

Brown, George T. and David E. Shi. *America: A Narrative History*. Seventh Edition. W.W. Norton & Company. 2007.

Halsey, William D. (Editorial Director). *Collier's Encyclopedia*. Crowell Collier and McMillian, Inc. 1966.

Josephy, Alvin M. Jr. *500 Nations: An Illustrated History of North American Indians*. Alfred A. Knopf. 1994.

Kutler, Stanley I. (Editor in Chief) *Dictionary of American History*. Third Edition. Thomson Gale. 2003.

Morison, Samuel E. *Admiral of the Ocean Sea: A Life of Christopher Columbus*. Little, Brown and Company. 1970.

Parry, John H. "Columbus, Christopher." *Encyclopedia Americana*. International Edition. Vol. 7, pp. 344-349. Americana Corporation. 1968.

Internet Reference

Weiner, Eric. "Coming to America: Who Was First?" October 8, 2007. Accessed December 27, 2019. https://www.npr.org/templates/story/story.php?storyid=15040888

Acknowledgements

I would like to thank Cynthia West and Lisa Zahn for their help in preparation of this book. All the photographs are from the public domain.

About the Author

Doug West is a retired engineer, small business owner, and experienced writer with several books to his credit. His writing interests are general, with expertise in science, history, and biographies. Doug has a B.S. in Physics from the Missouri School of Science and Technology and a Ph.D. in General Engineering from Oklahoma State University. He lives with his wife and little dog "Millie" near Kansas City, Missouri. Additional books by Doug West can be found at https://www.amazon.com/Doug-West/e/B00961PJ8M. Follow the author on Facebook at: https://www.facebook.com/30minutebooks.

Figure – Doug West (photo by Karina West)

Additional Books by Doug West

Buying and Selling Silver Bullion Like a Pro

How to Write, Publish, and Market Your Own Audio Book

A Short Biography of the Scientist Sir Isaac Newton

A Short Biography of the Astronomer Edwin Hubble

Galileo Galilei – A Short Biography

Benjamin Franklin – A Short Biography

The Astronomer Cecilia Payne-Gaposchkin – A Short Biography

The American Revolutionary War – A Short History

Coinage of the United States – A Short History

John Adams – A Short Biography

In the Footsteps of Columbus (Annotated) Introduction and Biography Included (with Annie J. Cannon)

Alexander Hamilton – Illustrated and Annotated (with Charles A. Conant)

Harlow Shapley – Biography of an Astronomer

Alexander Hamilton – A Short Biography

The Great Depression – A Short History

Jesse Owens, Adolf Hitler and the 1936 Summer Olympics

Thomas Jefferson – A Short Biography

Gold of My Father – A Short Tale of Adventure

Making Your Money Grow with Dividend Paying Stocks – Revised Edition

The French and Indian War – A Short History

The Mathematician John Forbes Nash Jr. – A Short Biography

The British Prime Minister Margaret Thatcher – A Short Biography

Vice President Mike Pence – A Short Biography

President Jimmy Carter – A Short Biography

President Ronald Reagan – A Short Biography

President George H. W. Bush – A Short Biography

Dr. Robert H. Goddard – A Brief Biography - Father of American Rocketry and the Space Age

Richard Nixon: A Short Biography - 37th President of the United States

Charles Lindbergh: A Short Biography - Famed Aviator and Environmentalist

Dr. Wernher von Braun: A Short Biography - Pioneer of Rocketry and Space Exploration

Bill Clinton: A Short Biography – 42nd President of the United States

Joe Biden: A Short Biography - 47th Vice President of the United States

Donald Trump: A Short Biography - 45th President of the United States

Nicolaus Copernicus: A Short Biography - The Astronomer Who Moved the Earth

America's Second War of Independence: A Short History of the War of 1812

John Quincy Adams: A Short Biography - Sixth President of the United States

Andrew Jackson: A Short Biography: Seventh President of the United States

Albert Einstein: A Short Biography Father of the Theory of Relativity

Franklin Delano Roosevelt: A Short Biography: Thirty-Second President of the United States

James Clerk Maxwell: A Short Biography: Giant of Nineteenth-Century Physics

Ernest Rutherford: A Short Biography: The Father of Nuclear Physics

Sir William Crookes: A Short Biography: Nineteenth-Century British Chemist and Spiritualist

The Journey of Apollo 11 to the Moon

William Henry Harrison: A Short Biography: Tenth President of the United States

John Tyler: A Short Biography: Eleventh President of the United States

James K. Polk: A Short Biography: Eleventh President of the United States

Louisa Catherine Adams: A Short Biography: First Lady of the United States

Samuel Adams: A Short Biography: Architect of the American Revolution

The Mexican-American War: A Short History: America's Fulfillment of Manifest Destiny

History of the Plymouth and Massachusetts Bay Colonies: Pilgrims, Puritans, and the Founding of New England

The History of the Jamestown Colony: America's First Permanent English Settlement

Zachary Taylor: A Short Biography: Twelfth President of the United States

Herbert Hoover: A Short Biography: Thirty-First President of the United States

The Great 1929 Stock Market Crash: A Short History

Index

Made in the USA
Monee, IL
30 August 2020

38803383R00049